D0854554

# THE OFFICIAL MANCHESTER UNITED ANNUAL 2010

Written by Steve Bartram and Gemma Thompson

A Grange Publication

© 2009. Published by Grange Communications Ltd., Edinburgh, under licence from Manchester United Football Club. Printed in the EU.

Every effort has been made to ensure the accuracy of information within this publication but the publishers cannot be held responsible for any errors or omissions. Views expressed are those of the authors and do not necessarily represent those of the publishers or the football club. All rights reserved.

Photographs © www.manutdpics.com

ISBN 978-1-907104-23-7

£6.99

# Contents

# Introduction

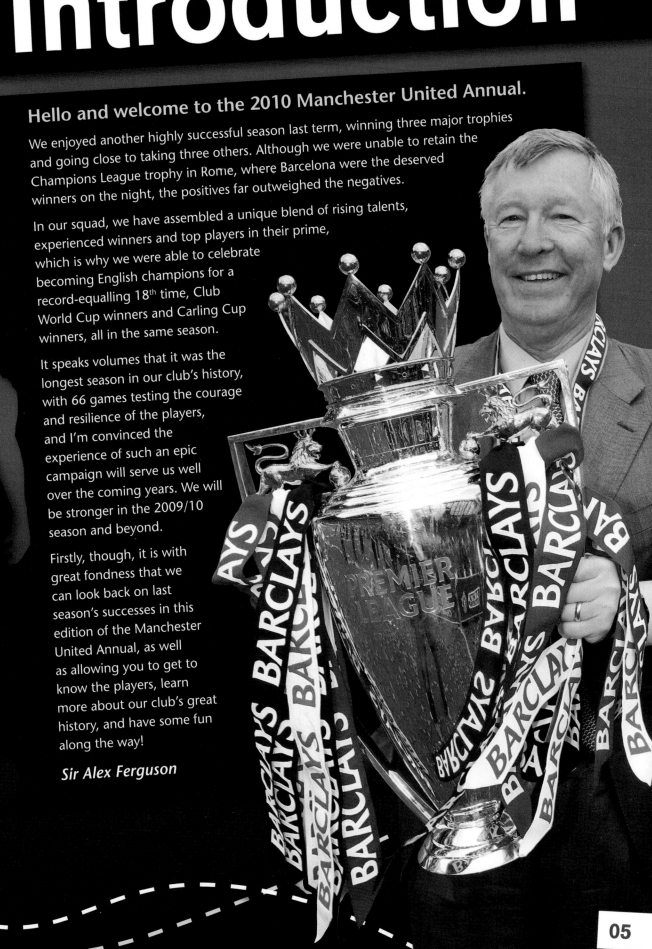

## Hello and welcome to the 2010 Manchester United Annual.

We enjoyed another highly successful season last term, winning three major trophies and going close to taking three others. Although we were unable to retain the Champions League trophy in Rome, where Barcelona were the deserved winners on the night, the positives far outweighed the negatives.

In our squad, we have assembled a unique blend of rising talents, experienced winners and top players in their prime, which is why we were able to celebrate becoming English champions for a record-equalling 18th time, Club World Cup winners and Carling Cup winners, all in the same season.

It speaks volumes that it was the longest season in our club's history, with 66 games testing the courage and resilience of the players, and I'm convinced the experience of such an epic campaign will serve us well over the coming years. We will be stronger in the 2009/10 season and beyond.

Firstly, though, it is with great fondness that we can look back on last season's successes in this edition of the Manchester United Annual, as well as allowing you to get to know the players, learn more about our club's great history, and have some fun along the way!

*Sir Alex Ferguson*

# 2008/09 Season Review

## ... told by the United players

### AUGUST 2008

The players' tale of the 2008/09 season begins with **Darren Fletcher**'s recollections of August, when the Reds began their defence of the Barclays Premier League title and contested two further cup finals...

"It was a tough start to the season. We gave everybody a head start and were playing catch-up after one game - a disappointing draw against Newcastle - but we'd been in that position before, so we knew that it was only day one of the season. We were raring to go for our next game, against Portsmouth, and we got a vital win at Fratton Park. I scored in both of those games, which was great personally because I'd been making a conscious effort to get into the box more often. We've got players who can put great balls in there, so if you keep getting in there, the law of averages says you're going to get a goal. From there we went to Monaco to contest the UEFA Super Cup against Zenit St Petersburg. We'd already won the Community Shield earlier in the month and we wanted to win another trophy. Unfortunately we lost to a top team, but it was still frustrating because this club's mentality is all about winning."

### Moment of the Month

After being frustrated by Portsmouth for 90 minutes at Wembley, the Reds retained the Community Shield with a comprehensive penalty shoot-out win, just as they had a year earlier against Chelsea. That triumph was the Reds' record-extending 17th win in the competition.

10/08/08 – Community Shield - United 0 Portsmouth 0 (United won 3-1 on penalties)
17/08/08 – Premier League - United 1 Newcastle 1 (Fletcher)
25/08/08 – Premier League – Portsmouth 0 United 1 (Fletcher)
29/08/08 – UEFA Super Cup Final – United 1 Zenit St Petersburg 2 (Vidic)

# SEPTEMBER 2008

September started as August had finished – with defeat – but **Ji-sung Park** says no-one ever panicked inside the United dressing room…

"Losing to Liverpool was very disappointing, but the mood amongst the players was still upbeat. We'd made a slow start to the season before but still ended up winning the Premier League and Champions League, so there was no need to worry and we all felt confident we could achieve the same again. I was really pleased to open the scoring at Chelsea and it was a very meaningful goal for me after being left out of the 2008 Champions League final. When the boss told me I'd be playing I knew it was a real opportunity to prove I'm good enough to play in the biggest games. It was only my third match back after knee surgery and I felt good. The month ended well for us with wins over Middlesbrough in the Carling Cup, Bolton in the league and Aalborg in the Champions League. I was really pleased for Berbatov to score his first United goals in Denmark. He's a brilliant player, very skilful and calm on the ball and he offers a different option going forward. There was a good feeling in the squad after that game – it was our third win in a row and we were determined to keep the momentum going."

## Moment of the month

Having spent over three quarters of United's clash with Bolton on the bench, Wayne Rooney was clearly keen to make up for lost time when he entered the fray on 71 minutes. Within six minutes he was on the score-sheet for the first time in 08/09, collecting Ronaldo's delicate backheel before cleverly creating space and caressing a gorgeous effort inside the far post.

13/09/08 – Premier League – Liverpool 2 United 1 (Tevez)
17/09/08 – Champions League – United 0 Villarreal 0
21/09/08 – Premier League – Chelsea 1 United 1 (Park)
23/09/08 – Carling Cup, Round 3 – United 3 Middlesbrough 1 (Ronaldo, Giggs, Nani)
27/09/08 – Premier League – United 2 Bolton 0 (Ronaldo, Rooney)
30/09/08 – Champions League – Aalborg 0 United 3 (Rooney, Berbatov 2)

# OCTOBER 2008

**Wayne Rooney scored three times during the month of October, as the Reds won four out of five games...**

"We normally hit form around the end of September and the beginning of October, and we managed to do that again. Personally, my goalscoring improved, but I'd not been doing anything differently to what I was doing at the start of the season – the only difference was that I was taking my chances. The manager left me out against Bolton in September and I wanted to show him what I could do. I like to prove people wrong if I can. After that I also scored at Blackburn, which has been a difficult place to go in recent years and the conditions weren't the best, but we got a great result. After that we had an international break, but everyone did really well in the first game back, against West Brom, and we fully deserved to win that game. The same went for the Celtic game, in which I was very proud to make my 200th United appearance, although it was frustrating to be held to a draw at Everton in the league after that. We bounced back against West Ham though, and everyone was talking about Berba's skills after that game. He's a great player and the mere fact he is at Old Trafford should take me onto a different level."

## Moment of the Month

Dimitar Berbatov displayed his stunning talents with an incredible piece of skill against West Ham. Seemingly struggling to keep the ball in play, the Bulgarian bypassed defender James Collins with two exquisite touches before setting up Ronaldo's second goal.

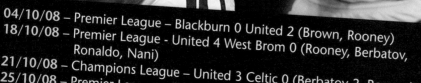

04/10/08 – Premier League – Blackburn 0 United 2 (Brown, Rooney)
18/10/08 – Premier League - United 4 West Brom 0 (Rooney, Berbatov, Ronaldo, Nani)
21/10/08 – Champions League – United 3 Celtic 0 (Berbatov 2, Rooney)
25/10/08 – Premier League – Everton 1 United 1 (Fletcher)
29/10/08 – Premier League – United 2 West Ham 0 (Ronaldo 2)

# NOVEMBER 2008

November brought a mixed bag of results, but **Nemanja Vidic** felt the Reds were moving in the right direction...

"We were pleased to start the month with victory over Hull, but we lost some poor goals. We shouldn't have let them back into the game and afterwards we were focused on learning from our mistakes and making sure they didn't happen again. I was pleased to get the fourth goal – I love that feeling when you score, especially as a defender, because it's not one of your main jobs. After the draw at Celtic, we travelled to Arsenal and played well. But yet again against one of our big rivals we didn't get the result. We'd not played too badly in any of the games against the top sides, but we'd conceded at vital times. I wasn't worried though because we'd shown we were not far away – we just needed that little bit of luck. We enjoyed a great win over Stoke at Old Trafford, but the goalless draw at Villa was very frustrating, especially as Liverpool and Chelsea also dropped points that day. When a team defends with 10 players behind the ball for the whole game, as Villa did, it's hard to create chances. We played very well at City a week later and thankfully Wayne got the winner which kept us in touch at the top of the table."

## Moment of the Month

It was fitting that Cristiano Ronaldo's 100th goal for the Reds, coming in the 5-0 thrashing of Stoke, should be one of his dead-ball specialities. After Tevez had been hacked down 30 yards from goal on three minutes, Ronaldo duly blasted a trademark rocket past Sorensen to bring up his century. Just for good measure, he later lashed home another for No.101.

01/11/08 – Premier League – United 4 Hull 3 (Ronaldo 2, Carrick, Vidic)
05/11/08 – Champions League – Celtic 1 United 1 (Giggs)
08/11/08 – Premier League – Arsenal 2 United 1 (Rafael)
11/11/08 – Carling Cup, Round 4 – United 1 QPR 0 (Tevez)
15/11/08 – Premier League – United 5 Stoke 0 (Ronaldo 2, Carrick, Berbatov, Welbeck)
22/11/08 – Premier League – Aston Villa 0 United 0
25/11/08 – Champions League – Villarreal 0 United 0
30/11/08 – Premier League – Manchester City 0 United 1 (Rooney)

# DECEMBER 2008

**Club captain Gary Neville returned from injury in December, a month in which United were crowned world champions and bagged some important league points...**

"I was happy to be back playing during December, as I'd had a few injuries over the previous few months. It was a relief to play against Blackburn, where Carlos Tevez was superb and scored four goals to send us through. From there, much of the month was taken up by the Club World Cup. We had an important late win against Sunderland and draws against Aalborg and Tottenham before we went, and once we were over in Japan we were intent on winning the trophy. We got a little sloppy in the semi-final against Gamba Osaka but progressed, and then beat Liga de Quito in the final thanks to a goal from Wayne. 2008 had been a great year already, but winning in Japan topped it off, although we couldn't dwell on that because we were straight back into a game at Stoke on Boxing Day. We had to be patient, but Carlos was there to put the chance away when it finally came along. Stoke are a huge team, but we're a tough team to play against, both in attack and defence, and we never shirk anything. After that came a narrow, but vital, win over Middlesbrough, which meant we rounded the year off nicely."

### Moment of the Month

Wayne Rooney may have won the Club World Cup in Japan, but Sir Alex Ferguson later identified Carlos Tevez's winner at Stoke as the season's most important goal. With United's players jetlagged and time ticking away, the Argentine popped up with a priceless close-range winner to kick-start the Reds' title challenge.

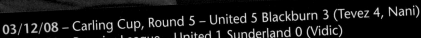

03/12/08 – Carling Cup, Round 5 – United 5 Blackburn 3 (Tevez 4, Nani)
06/12/08 – Premier League – United 1 Sunderland 0 (Vidic)
10/12/08 – Champions League – United 2 Aalborg 2 (Tevez, Rooney)
13/12/08 – Premier League – Tottenham 0 United 0
18/12/08 – Club World Cup Semi-final – Gamba Osaka 3 United 5 (Vidic, Ronaldo, Fletcher, Rooney 2)
21/12/08 – Club World Cup Final – United 1 Liga de Quito 0 (Rooney)
26/12/08 – Premier League – Stoke 0 United 1 (Tevez)
29/12/08 – Premier League – United 1 Middlesbrough 0 (Berbatov)

## JANUARY 2009

January turned out to be a memorable month as United went top for the first time and **Edwin van der Sar** rewrote the history books...

"Starting a new year with a win is always a good feeling. It took us a while to settle in the FA Cup tie against Southampton and we got a bit of luck with the first goal when it came back off the crossbar to Danny Welbeck, but in the end we deserved the win and could have scored more. We had a great win over Chelsea and followed that with another important three points against Wigan, which was the first of our two games in hand. Berba's injury-time winner at Bolton sent us top for the first time in the season. It felt very satisfying, if a little surprising – we were quite a way behind when we got back from Japan, but we'd managed to make up a lot of points in a few weeks. The win at West Brom was a particularly special night for me as it was my 11th clean sheet which beat Petr Cech's previous record. I remember watching the minutes tick away towards the end and even though we were a few goals up I still felt very nervous. It was a proud moment when the final whistle sounded, but you can't achieve things on your own because everyone in the team plays their part. The record was a bonus really, the main thing was we were getting the results we needed and it was important we kept the form going because we all knew it could lead to bigger things at the end of the season."

### Moment of the Month

Past servants aside, never before has the Old Trafford faithful afforded such a warm welcome to an opposition player than that reserved for John Terry. It was the Chelsea skipper's first visit to M16 since Moscow and how he must have been dreading it. Ironic cheers rang round the stadium when his name was read out before the game and greeted his every touch. United's 3-0 win was merely the icing on the cake.

04/01/09 – FA Cup, Round 3 – Southampton 0 United 3 (Welbeck, Nani, Gibson)
07/01/09 – Carling Cup Semi-final 1 – Derby 1 United 0
11/01/09 – Premier League – United 3 Chelsea 0 (Vidic, Rooney, Berbatov)
14/01/09 – Premier League – United 1 Wigan 0 (Rooney)
17/01/09 – Premier League – Bolton 0 United 1 (Berbatov)
20/01/09 – Carling Cup Semi-final 2 – United 4 Derby 2, agg 4-3 (Nani, O'Shea, Tevez, Ronaldo)
24/01/09 – FA Cup, Round 4 – United 2 Tottenham 1 (Scholes, Berbatov)
27/01/09 – Premier League – West Brom 0 United 5 (Berbatov, Tevez, Vidic, Ronaldo 2)
31/01/09 – Premier League – United 1 Everton 0 (Ronaldo)

# FEBRUARY 2009

**Ryan Giggs, who became PFA Player of the Year for the first time in his epic playing career, hit top form as United continued to fight on three fronts during February...**

"I was really glad to start February with the winner against West Ham and it was quite rare to score with my right foot. As my career has worn on I've enjoyed my football more than ever, and I was delighted to sign a new one-year contract shortly after the win at Upton Park. I love being part of an exciting young team with great dressing room spirit and I played with a few of the young lads in the FA Cup win at Derby. It's up to the players like Gary Neville, Edwin van der Sar and myself to pass on our experience to the lads who come in - the likes of Darron Gibson and Danny Welbeck, who scored fantastic goals at Pride Park. There were more personnel changes to the team as we beat Fulham and Blackburn at Old Trafford, before a frustrating Champions League game at Inter. We completely outplayed them, and it was just a shame we couldn't score that all-important away goal. Still, we felt confident and that showed in our performance, so we were looking forward to our next game – the Carling Cup Final against Spurs."

## Moment of the Month
After Giggsy had rolled back the years with his performance at West Ham, Paul Scholes served a timely reminder of his own enduring importance with a passing masterclass against Fulham, capped by a stunning long-range volley direct from a corner.

08/02/09 – Premier League – West Ham 0 United 1 (Giggs)
15/02/09 – FA Cup, Round 5 – Derby 1 United 4 (Nani, Gibson, Ronaldo, Welbeck)
18/02/09 – Premier League – United 3 Fulham 0 (Scholes, Berbatov, Rooney)
21/02/09 – Premier League – United 2 Blackburn 1 (Rooney, Ronaldo)
24/02/09 – Champions League Knock-out round 1 – Internazionale 0 United 0

# MARCH 2009

**Rio Ferdinand** skippered the Reds to Carling Cup glory at the beginning of the month, but Liverpool and Fulham ensured it ended in a very different fashion...

"Lifting the Carling Cup was one of the proudest moments of my career and a great way to start the month. Ironically, I didn't even expect to be playing, I only found out on the morning of the game, so it all fell into place brilliantly for me. From there, we picked up a hard-fought win at Newcastle and produced a fantastic performance at Fulham in the FA Cup. Unfortunately, I went off at half-time after injuring my ankle. I've never really had many injuries, but last season was the first time I've had runs of missing a few games at a time which was very frustrating. Thankfully, in this instance, I was fit for our next match against Inter and even though we didn't play as well as in the first leg, we got the job done. Unfortunately things didn't go to plan against Liverpool. Losing any game is disappointing, losing to your big rivals is even worse and the scoreline compounded that. The quicker you bounce back from a setback the better, but we just didn't perform at Fulham a week later. It certainly gave us a rude awakening and we knew it was up to us to turn things around."

## Moment of the Month

Injuries and the form of Edwin van der Sar may have forced Ben Foster to bide his time, but when he was finally handed his chance to shine in the Carling Cup final at Wembley, he didn't disappoint. Vital stops from Lennon and Bent in normal and extra-time were followed by an excellent penalty save from O'Hara in the shoot-out, before Anderson fired the clincher.

01/03/09 – Carling Cup Final – United 0 Tottenham 0 (United won 4-1 on pens)
04/03/09 – Premier League – Newcastle 1 United 2 (Rooney, Berbatov)
07/03/09 – FA Cup, Round 6 – Fulham 0 United 4 (Tevez 2, Rooney, Park)
11/03/09 – Champions League Knock-out round 2 – United 2 Internazionale 0, agg 2-0 (Vidic, Ronaldo)
14/03/09 – Premier League – United 1 Liverpool 4 (Ronaldo)
21/03/09 – Premier League – Fulham 2 United 0

# APRIL 2009

After a difficult end to March, April proved to be a pivotal month in the season for **Michael Carrick** and his United colleagues…

"We'd gone so long without a league defeat, that when we lost to Liverpool and Fulham it was a bit of a shock to the system. The key was how we bounced back, and the game against Aston Villa was a huge victory – the winner from Kiko Macheda was one of those moments where you immediately recognise its importance. Getting a victory that day gave everyone a massive lift, although we were understandably a bit drained when we played Porto two days later. We were able to get through the second leg with a really good team performance and a brilliant goal from Cristiano. I've seen him do it so many times in training, but it was great for him to save one for a big game! We weren't as impressive at Sunderland, but sometimes it's the games you come through when you are not at your best that give you the best feeling. It's also nice to chip in with the odd goal, which I did against Portsmouth. That followed a disappointing FA Cup exit, but we ended April on a high against Arsenal. We should have scored more but we always believed we could finish the job at the Emirates in May."

## Moment of the Month

In a month of outstanding goals and games, nothing could rival Kiko Macheda's debut winner against Aston Villa. The 17-year-old Italian curled home a stunning injury-time winner to snare three vital points and propel United towards the Premier League title.

05/04/09 – Premier League – United 3 Aston Villa 2 (Ronaldo 2, Macheda)
07/04/09 – Champions League Quarter-final 1 – United 2 Porto 2 (Rooney, Tevez)
11/04/09 – Premier League – Sunderland 1 United 2 (Scholes, Macheda)
15/04/09 – Champions League Quarter-final 2 – Porto 0 United 1, agg 2-3 (Ronaldo)
19/04/09 – FA Cup Semi-final – Everton 0 United 0, (Everton won 4-2 on penalties)
22/04/09 – Premier League – United 2 Portsmouth 0 (Rooney, Carrick)
25/04/09 – Premier League – United 5 Tottenham 2 (Ronaldo 2, Rooney 2, Berbatov)
29/04/09 – Champions League Semi-final 1 - United 1 Arsenal 0 (O'Shea)

## 2008/09 Season Review

**Patrice Evra reflects on a bittersweet final month as the Reds continued the fight for silverware at home and abroad…**

"It's always a privilege to play for this club, especially when you are battling for trophies and have the opportunity to make history. There may be a lot of pressure involved, but it's a pressure I'm happy to have. Our victory at Middlesbrough kept us on course for the title and we followed that with a fantastic performance against Arsenal to reach the Champions League final; tactically and technically we were far superior. The only bad news was Fletch's sending off. I felt so frustrated for him, particularly as I'd been worrying about missing the final if I picked up another booking. We had to put Rome to the back of our minds and thankfully we followed up with two vital wins over City and Wigan. A draw with Arsenal was enough to secure a third successive title and it was very special to win it in front of our fans. Thoughts soon turned to Rome and a lot of people were asking me how I felt about facing Lionel Messi – the simple answer was very confident, but I knew I'd need to work hard, we all knew that. Unfortunately, Barcelona were the better team and deserved to win. It was one of the most disappointing nights of my career, but it's important to remember the positives of a really great season."

### Moment of the Month

Having already taken a 2-0 lead in their Champions League visit to the Emirates, the Reds saved the best 'til last with a sweeping move of devastating nature. Vidic's headed clearance was backheeled by Ronaldo into the path of Park, who spotted Rooney bursting forward. He in turn slipped a pass to the onrushing Ronaldo, who calmly guided the ball into the roof of the net. Simply stunning.

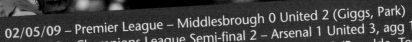

02/05/09 – Premier League – Middlesbrough 0 United 2 (Giggs, Park)
05/05/09 – Champions League Semi-final 2 – Arsenal 1 United 3, agg 1-4 (Park, Ronaldo 2)
10/05/09 – Premier League – United 2 Manchester City 0 (Ronaldo, Tevez)
13/05/09 – Premier League – Wigan 1 United 2 (Tevez, Carrick)
16/05/09 – Premier League – United 0 Arsenal 0
24/05/09 – Premier League – Hull 0 United 1 (Gibson)
27/05/09 – Champions League Final – Barcelona 2 United 0

# Party time

16

# Player Profiles

## GOALKEEPERS

### Edwin van der Sar

**Born:** 29 October 1970; Voorhout, Holland
**Previous Clubs:** Ajax, Juventus, Fulham
**Joined United:** 1 July 2005
**United Debut:** 9 August 2005 vs Debreceni (H),
UEFA Champions League
**International Team:** Holland (retired)

His 40th birthday may loom on the horizon, but Dutch stopper Edwin van der Sar continues to raise the bar. The giant goalkeeper has been a cornerstone of the team since his arrival from Fulham, and followed his penalty shootout heroics in Moscow with a record-breaking run of clean sheets during the 2008/09 season.

**He says:** *"It's a great club to be at, with a great atmosphere in the dressing room, the boss is fantastic and we have the best stadium in England."*

### Ben Foster

**Born:** 3 April 1983; Leamington Spa
**Previous Clubs:** Stoke City, Bristol City (loan), Kidderminster (loan), Wrexham (loan), Watford (loan)
**Joined United:** 19 July 2005
**United Debut:** 15 March 2008 vs Derby County (A), Premier League
**International Team:** England

Ben Foster had to be patient for his competitive Reds debut after spending two successful seasons on loan at Watford. Injuries and the form of Edwin van der Sar have somewhat restricted his progress, but there is no doubt he has a bright future ahead at Old Trafford, and on the international stage.

**He says:** *"My future is all down to Sir Alex. I put my trust in him and whatever he decides to do will be the right thing for the club and for my development as a player."*

### Tomasz Kuszczak

**Born:** 20 March 1982; Krosno Odrzanskie, Poland
**Previous Clubs:** Hertha Berlin, West Bromwich Albion
**Joined United:** 10 August 2006
**United Debut:** 17 September 2006 vs Arsenal (H), Premier League
**International Team:** Poland

Although he has only made a small number of appearances across his three seasons at Old Trafford, Tomasz has played several key cameo roles in the Reds' repeated successes. An able deputy whenever called upon, Tomasz has some of the key attributes in any good goalkeeper – particularly excellent reflexes and agility.

**He says:** *"It can be tough when you're not first-choice, but you always need to be ready in case you're needed."*

# Rio Ferdinand

Born: 7 November 1978; Peckham
Previous Clubs: West Ham, Bournemouth (loan), Leeds United
Joined United: 22 July 2002
United Debut: 27 August 2002 vs Zalaegerszeg (H), UEFA Champions League
International Team: England

Rio Ferdinand is one of the finest defenders in world football. Armed with elegance, pace and an astute ability to read the game, he has grown into one of United and England's most influential performers, while his leadership qualities have seen him made captain for club and country on numerous occasions. After swapping Elland Road for Old Trafford in the summer of 2002, Ferdinand helped the Reds wrestle the championship crown from Arsenal in his first season. Since then, he has played a prominent role – often as skipper, invariably as part of an imposing partnership with Nemanja Vidic - as United have swept three successive Premier League titles.

He says: "All the work I've done in my career, all the hard progress I've made, has been about being the best player I can be. I want to fulfil every bit of my potential."

# Nemanja Vidic

Born: 21 October 1981; Uzice, Serbia
Previous Clubs: Red Star Belgrade, Spartak Moscow
Joined United: 5 January 2006
United Debut: 25 January 2006 vs Blackburn Rovers (H), League Cup
International Team: Serbia

Having arrived at Old Trafford as a virtual unknown from Spartak Moscow, central defender Nemanja Vidic quickly set about making friends with United fans by virtue of his no-nonsense approach to defending. It's safe to say that opposing strikers never relish coming up against the hard-as-nails Serbian, who has established himself as one of the world's top defenders during his time at Old Trafford. He has improved season-by-season, and was utterly outstanding last season as the Reds' success was built on solid defensive foundations.

He says: "To be playing for United, the biggest club in England and probably the world, is an absolute honour."

# Wes Brown

Born: 13 October 1979; Manchester
Previous Clubs: Trainee
Joined United: 8 July 1996
United Debut: 4 May 1998 vs Leeds (H), Premier League
International Team: England

A tough-tackling, no-nonsense defender capable of playing in the centre or on the right, Wes Brown is one of the Reds' most dedicated servants. Despite winning almost every club medal in the game, the Manchester-born defender has not been so fortunate on the injury front, thanks to a string of long-term lay-offs which have punctuated his career. A strong and resolute character, Wes has never let himself be beaten, however, and he enjoyed arguably his finest season in a red shirt in 2007/08, replacing the long-term injured Gary Neville at right-back on the way to helping United to double glory. Injury again ravaged Brown's 2008/09 campaign, but he remains an integral part of Sir Alex Ferguson's plans.

He says: "I've grown up at United, I've developed my career here and I'm delighted to play football here – it's the best club in the world."

# Gary Neville

Born: 18 February 1975; Bury
Previous Clubs: Trainee
Joined United: 8 July 1991
United Debut: 16 September 1992 vs Torpedo Moscow (H), UEFA Cup
International Team: England

The Bury-born right-back is as loyal a servant as any team could hope to have. A Red through and through, he is among a dying breed of one-club men, having joined United as a teenager. Vocal and single-minded, the current club captain has all the attributes and characteristics of a great leader who gives his all in every game, demanding the same from his team-mates. A member of the famous 1992 Youth Cup-winning side, Neville has over 550 appearances and numerous winners' medals under his belt and belongs to an elite group of players who have skippered the Reds to the Premier League title.

**He says:** *"I still get the same buzz playing for United now that I did when I started out."*

# John O'Shea

Born: 30 April 1981; Waterford, Ireland
Previous Clubs: Trainee, Bournemouth (loan), Royal Antwerp (loan)
Joined United: 3 August 1998
United Debut: 13 October 1999 vs Aston Villa (A), League Cup
International Team: Republic of Ireland

An astute reader of the game and versatile enough to perform naturally in a variety of positions, John O'Shea is winning the respect he deserves as he reaches a decade of first team football at Old Trafford. True, he has played in almost every position in Sir Alex's side, but the big Irishman has increasingly honed his role as a full-back who can operate on either flank. His knack for popping up with vital goals is just another reason why he has become an indispensable member of the squad.

**He says:** *"It'd be nice, at some stage, to pin down a position but the most important thing at this club is that you play and do whatever you're asked to."*

# Rafael da Silva

Born: 9 July 1990; Rio de Janeiro, Brazil
Previous Club: Fluminense
Joined United: 1 July 2008
United Debut: 17 August 2008 vs Newcastle (H), Premier League
International Team: Brazil (youth)

"His enthusiasm and the adventurous way he plays is typical of a Manchester United player," commented Sir Alex Ferguson following Rafael da Silva's exciting debut season. The epitome of the modern full-back, he, and twin brother Fabio, were spotted by Reds' scouts in the summer of 2005 at a Hong Kong youth tournament. They had to wait over a year for international clearance on their transfer, but both looked the part from the start. Despite competition from Neville and Brown at various stages of the season, Rafael continually proved his ability to cope with high pressure matches with a calmness that belied his tender years and suggested a very bright future.

**He says:** *"I love this club. I am already thinking of being here for many, many years."*

## Fabio da Silva

**Born:** 9 July 1990; Rio de Janeiro, Brazil
**Previous Club:** Fluminense
**Joined United:** 1 July 2008
**United Debut:** 24 January 2009 vs Tottenham Hotspur (H), FA Cup
**International Team:** Brazil (youth)

Just like his twin brother, Rafael, Fabio da Silva is a tremendously skilled young full-back who has represented his native Brazil at youth international level. Since arriving at Old Trafford from Fluminense in 2008, Fabio has endured more injury frustration than his brother, but remains a hot prospect for the near future. Fabio is a calm, considered defender who can also lend breathless support in attack, while he is also particularly adept from free-kicks.

**He says:** *"The mentality at United is like it is with Brazil. If you win but don't play well, nobody is happy. I'm very happy to be here with great players who all want to win by playing well."*

## Jonny Evans

**Born:** 2 January 1988; Belfast, Northern Ireland
**Previous Clubs:** Trainee, Royal Antwerp (loan), Sunderland (loan)
**Joined United:** 1 July 2004
**United Debut:** 26 September 2007 vs Coventry City (H), League Cup
**International Team:** Northern Ireland

Following his rise through the Old Trafford youth ranks, Jonny has blossomed into one of the most promising young central defenders around, with Sir Alex admitting: "His United future is assured." A season on loan at Sunderland allowed the Northern Ireland international to gain valuable experience and hone his skills, both of which he was able to call upon when he returned to United at the beginning of 2008/09 and was plunged in at the deep end against Villarreal and Chelsea. He carried out his defensive duties against both with aplomb, as he did throughout his 34 appearances, five of which came during the Reds' record-breaking clean sheet run.

**He says:** *"As a defender, I try to win my battles and then play it simple, to allow some of the best players in the world to attack."*

## Patrice Evra

**Born:** 15 May 1981; Dakar, Senegal
**Previous Clubs:** Masala, Monza, Monaco
**Joined United:** 10 January 2006
**United Debut:** 14 January 2006 vs Manchester City (A), Premier League
**International Team:** France

Just watching United's first choice left-back can be a breathless experience. It took him a few months to settle in England after arriving from Monaco, but he soon ousted fans' favourite Gabriel Heinze and made himself part of the first team furniture at United. Pat quickly endeared himself to United supporters with his tough tackling and non-stop running, and his bombarding runs down the left flank never fail to set the Old Trafford crowd buzzing in anticipation.

**He says:** *"What has struck me since getting to United is the fact that I'm at a big club and also at a big family."*

# MIDFIELDERS

## Paul Scholes

**Born:** 16 November 1974; Salford
**Previous Clubs:** Trainee
**Joined United:** 8 July 1991
**United Debut:** 21 September 1994 v Port Vale (A), League Cup
**International Team:** England (retired)

Despite his relative seniority, Paul Scholes' underlying quality remains intact. Part of the new wave of talent that ushered in Beckham, Giggs, Butt and the Nevilles in the mid-1990s, the shy, modest midfielder scored twice on his debut at Port Vale – and on his first league outing against Ipswich – and has never looked back. A player who has the ability to control a game in the simplest of fashions, he also has a deadly eye for goal both inside and outside the box. Now in the all-time top four appearance-makers at the club, Scholes is, indisputably, one of the finest talents in United's history.

**He says:** *"I've been very lucky to play for a great club who happen to be my local club."*

## Michael Carrick

**Born:** 28 July 1981; Wallsend
**Previous Clubs:** West Ham, Swindon (loan), Birmingham (loan), Tottenham Hotspur
**Joined United:** 31 July 2006
**United Debut:** 23 August 2006 vs Charlton Athletic (A), Premier League
**International Team:** England

Since arriving from Spurs, Michael Carrick has evolved into one of the most complete, cultured midfielders in Europe. He has benefited enormously from playing and training alongside Paul Scholes, one of the finest playmakers in the modern era, and Michael has realised his potential of dictating the tempo of matches. Comfortable in tight spots and with the ball on either foot, he can unlock the tightest of defences and has also added far more goals to his game than he had mustered at his previous clubs.

**He says:** *"It was a big challenge to come to a place like this and learn to become a better player. I've certainly done that and to win trophies as well has been great."*

## Darren Fletcher

**Born:** 1 February 1984; Edinburgh, Scotland
**Previous Clubs:** Trainee
**Joined United:** 3 July 2000
**United Debut:** 12 March 2003 vs FC Basel (H), UEFA Champions League
**International Team:** Scotland

Perhaps United's most improved player over recent seasons. Fletch has evolved into one of the most effective big-game players around, and his boundless energy often has opponents hassled into submission. Darren broke into the United team at a young age – Sir Alex even tried to field him when he was just 16 – and after years of steady improvement, he has developed into a top class player. With his intelligent reading of the game, efficient passing and non-stop running, Fletch is a key component of United's midfield, and a vital weapon in stopping opponents.

**He says:** *"I try and get on the ball, trying to control the game and make things happen."*

# Owen Hargreaves

Born: 20 January 1981; Calgary, Canada
Previous Club: Bayern Munich
Joined United: 1 July 2007
United Debut: 19 August 2007 vs Manchester City (A), Premier League
International Team: England

Owen Hargreaves brings vast experience to United's midfield, as well as a determined, energetic and enthusiastic style. Unfortunately for the England international, a spate of injuries has prevented him from exerting his influence on a consistent basis since joining the Reds from Bayern Munich, where he won four Bundesliga titles and the Champions League. One of the most highly-regarded defensive midfielders in the game, Hargreaves produced a string of tireless performances during the 2007/08 double-winning campaign and was a scorer in the Champions League final penalty shoot-out victory over Chelsea in Moscow.

**He says:** "My favourite position is in that holding role, getting stuck in and winning tackles and laying it off. Those are the things I can bring to a team."

# Anderson

Born: 13 April 1988; Porto Alegre, Brazil
Previous Clubs: Gremio, FC Porto
Joined United: 1 July 2007
United Debut: 1 September 2007 vs Sunderland (H), Premier League
International Team: Brazil

Few people had heard of Anderson Luis de Abreu Oliveira when he arrived in July 2007, but having been billed as the 'new Ronaldinho' expectations were certainly high. In truth, he's actually quite different to his international team-mate; where Ronaldinho is flicks and flamboyance, Ando, as he's known to his team-mates, is brimming with energy and industry. A bubbly character on and off the pitch, he is also more than capable of dealing with high pressure situations as he proved with successful penalty conversions in the 2008 Champions League final and 2009 Carling Cup final shoot-outs.

**He says:** "I find it difficult to describe how it feels to hear the fans sing my name – it's amazing. It gives me extra strength on the pitch."

# Darron Gibson

Born: 25 October 1987; Derry, Northern Ireland
Previous Clubs: Trainee, Royal Antwerp (loan), Wolves (loan)
Joined United: 1 July 2004
United Debut: 26 October 2005 vs Barnet (H), League Cup
International Team: Republic of Ireland

It looked like Darron may have missed the boat after he found himself loaned out to Wolves during the 2007/08 campaign, two seasons after making his first-team debut, but he has since exposed himself as a talented young midfielder who can graft and create in equal measure. Already a full Republic of Ireland international, Gibbo, as he is known to his team-mates, is blessed with two good feet, a tremendous eye for a pass and some ferocious shooting.

**He says:** "My overall game is improving every day because I am working with the best players in the world."

# Zoran Tosic

Born: 28 April 1987; Zrenjanin, Serbia
Previous Clubs: Proleter Zrenjanin, Banat Zrenjanin, Partizan Belgrade
Joined United: 2 January 2009
United Debut: 24 January 2009 vs Tottenham (H), FA Cup
International Team: Serbia

While not a world star when United signed him from Partizan Belgrade in January 2009, Zoran Tosic was already a familiar name at Carrington thanks to over a year of extensive research by the club's scouts. A left-winger who hugs the touchline and takes on defenders, he possesses silky dribbling skills and a strong left-foot shot. Renowned for his mastery in dead-ball situations, the Serbian international is a real threat from set-pieces, whether firing goalwards or delivering pin-point crosses. A United fan since childhood, Tosic is aiming to follow in his heroes' footsteps and become an Old Trafford favourite.

**He says:** *"I want to become a top player at United and not waste the opportunity of being a member of the greatest football family."*

# Nani

Born: 17 November 1986; Praia, Cape Verde
Previous Club: Sporting Lisbon
Joined United: 1 July 2007
United Debut: 5 August 2007 vs Chelsea (N), Community Shield
International Team: Portugal

A skilful and pacy winger who can play on either flank, Luís Carlos Almeida da Cunha (or Nani, as we all call him) arrived at Old Trafford as one of the most promising young players in Europe when he joined from Sporting Lisbon in the summer of 2007. The man touted as 'the next Cristiano Ronaldo' got his United career off to a spectacular start with a stunning winner (and trademark acrobatic celebration) against Tottenham on his fifth appearance. Three more goals followed that season, as did a vital penalty conversion in the Champions League final shoot-out in Moscow. Opportunities were harder to come by in his second term, but there's no doubting his speed, skill and scoring potential.

**He says:** *"I think I have improved a lot since I joined United. And as I get more games, more training and more time learning, I will keep on improving as a player."*

**Born:** 25 February 1981; Seoul, South Korea
**Previous Clubs:** Kyoto Purple Sanga, PSV Eindhoven
**Joined United:** 8 July 2005
**United Debut:** 9 August 2005 vs Debreceni (H), UEFA Champions League
**International Team:** South Korea

The first Korean to play for United, Ji-sung Park is a fans' favourite for his tremendous work ethic, vision and movement. He has gathered nicknames such as 'three-lung Park', such is his vigorous approach to the game – he never gives opponents a moment's peace. Ji arrived from PSV Eindhoven in the summer of 2005, and has been steadily improving his game, year after year. He openly admits that he would like to score more often but, with his intelligent reading of the game and phenomenal stamina, there's no doubt they will start to flow.

**He says:** *"I hope I've shown the way for other young players in South Korea, that they too can come and play football in Europe."*

## Ryan Giggs

**Born:** 29 November 1973; Cardiff, Wales
**Previous Clubs:** Trainee
**Joined United:** 9 July 1990
**United Debut:** 2 March 1991 vs Everton (H), First Division
**International Team:** Wales (retired)

Having made his debut over 18 years ago, Ryan has built up a legendary United career which has seen him become the most decorated player in British football history, and also become the club's record appearance maker. He has played over 800 games under Sir Alex, and overtook the previous record holder, Sir Bobby Charlton, in the 2008 Champions League final. Whereas he began his career as a dashing young left winger, Ryan has gradually evolved into a more central role, where his close control, movement and vision continue to make him one of the most potent weapons in United's arsenal.

**He says:** *"I've been at United since I was 13 and I'm very fond of the club and the fans; they have been an integral part of my life."*

## Dimitar Berbatov

**Born:** 30 January 1981; Blagoevgrad, Bulgaria
**Previous Clubs:** CSKA Sofia, Bayer Leverkusen, Tottenham
**Joined United:** 1 September 2008
**United Debut:** 13 September 2008 vs Liverpool (A), Premier League
**International Team:** Bulgaria

There is no doubting Dimitar Berbatov's qualities as a goalscorer and provider for others. A classy and complete centre-forward with the ability to ruthlessly and regularly find the net inside the box, he also possesses the rare talent to conjure moments of sheer magic outside it. Just as a certain mercurial Frenchman could single-handedly change the flow of a game, Berba is equally capable of following suit. And, like Cantona, he shares a happy knack for scoring important goals, as Middlesbrough and Bolton found to their cost midway through 2008/09, which proved to be a promising debut campaign from the Bulgarian.

**He says:** *"Personally, this is the best squad I've been involved with. It's a pleasure just to be here and follow in the footsteps of so many great players."*

## Wayne Rooney

**Born:** 24 October 1985; Liverpool
**Previous Club:** Everton
**Joined United:** 31 August 2004
**United Debut:** 28 September 2004 vs Fenerbahce (H), UEFA Champions League
**International Team:** England

The England striker burst to prominence in 2002 when, aged just 16, he scored a superb winner against reigning champions Arsenal for his boyhood club Everton. He soon established himself on the international scene, and was prised away from Goodison Park in 2004 for £28million. Wayne scored a hat-trick on his United debut against Fenerbahce, and became an instant Old Trafford hero. Six seasons on, his status as a fans' favourite remains unbreakable, as his passionate approach, non-stop running and sublime skills make him an utterly indispensable part of Sir Alex's team, and arguably England's finest talent.

**He says:** *"Everything I do, I want to win, whether that's playing PlayStation or playing at Old Trafford."*

## Federico Macheda

Born: 22 August 1991; Rome, Italy
Previous Club: Lazio
Joined United: 1 September 2007
United Debut: 5 April 2009 vs Aston Villa (H), Premier League
International Team: Italy (youth)

Young Italian striker Federico 'Kiko' Macheda arrived at Old Trafford from Lazio in the summer of 2007 and quickly became a key member of the club's under-18s side. He swiftly rose through the ranks to the Reserves because of his superb goalscoring, and he continued to regularly find the net with the Reds' second string. He thrived under manager Ole Gunnar Solskjaer, and was promoted to first team duties in April 2009. A virtual unknown to most supporters inside Old Trafford when he made his debut against Aston Villa, Kiko quickly became a terrace idol with a superb injury-time winner. A typical Italian striker in terms of his penalty area prowess, Kiko also boasts the physical toughness to make the grade in England.

**He says:** *"I am very proud to call myself a United player. You're playing for probably the best team in the world."*

## Danny Welbeck

Born: 26 November 1990; Manchester
Previous Clubs: Trainee
Joined United: 1 July 2007
United Debut: 23 September 2008 vs Middlesbrough (H), League Cup
International Team: England (youth)

The Manchester-born attacker was an early learner at Old Trafford after starting out for the under-11's. A tricky forward with pace, skill and strength on the ball, he quickly progressed through the ranks. After spending the second half of the 2007/08 campaign mixing with the first team in training, he made the full step up at the start of 2008/09. In only his second game, a Carling Cup tie against QPR, he won the match-winning penalty, and four days later scored one of the goals of the season on his league debut against Stoke. There's plenty more to come and working alongside the likes of Rooney, Owen and Berbatov will help him no end.

**He says:** *"Scoring in front of the Stretford End is what every young boy from Manchester dreams of."*

# New for 2009/10

## Michael Owen

The most surprising addition to United's squad during the summer of 2009 was unquestionably Michael Owen. Plucked from limbo on a free transfer after suffering relegation with his former club, Newcastle, the England striker was quick to outline his plans for a bright future at Old Trafford...

**Name:** Michael Owen
**Position:** Striker
**Born:** 14 December 1979, Chester, England
**Previous Clubs:** Liverpool, Real Madrid, Newcastle United

**Michael, how did it feel to sign for Manchester United?**
It felt great. I never even had it in my wildest dreams really but then I got the call from the manager to come and meet him. It was a shock but I'm obviously really happy and things moved quickly from then.

**At the end of last season, did you think you'd be playing for United this season?**
No, but I've been here in the past. I came here a couple of times as a kid, and I played in a tournament up north for United. I met the manager and even in the last few years, you speak to players and other people, I had an idea that the manager still thought I had something. I probably had a poor spell up at Newcastle but prior to that, my career was very good and I'm sure a top club like this can reignite my career.

**How much have you enjoyed playing alongside the other lads so far?**
It's been great. As soon as you sign, you think, I'm going to start playing football with some top players who have great experience. There are fantastic players throughout the squad and that's why they've all won so much in their careers so far. Hopefully I can jump on the bandwagon, score a few goals and obviously help us to achieve further success.

**What do you hope to achieve here?**
When you think about United, you automatically think about winning trophies, the stadium and the massive fan base. Until you sign, you don't let yourself get carried away. But there's a lot to think about - all the top players that are here, the manager, the fans, the atmosphere at Old Trafford and everything else about the club.

## Mame Biram Diouf

**Name:** Mame Biram Diouf
**Position:** Striker
**Born:** 16 December 1987; Dakar, Senegal
**Previous Clubs:** Diaraf, Molde FK

United had hoped to secure the signing of Mame Biram Diouf later in his career, but growing interest from other clubs in the Senegal youth international prompted decisive action from the Reds in July 2009. Plucked from Norway's Molde FK - just like club legend Ole Gunnar Solskjaer - Mame is a powerful young striker who averaged a goal every two games during his time in Norway. Upon completing his move, Diouf said: "Playing for Manchester has always been a dream of mine ever since I was a small boy. I am confident of playing very well."

# Antonio Valencia

Following the departure of Cristiano Ronaldo, Sir Alex Ferguson's first move was designed to replace the winger's trickery and knack of supplying goals, hence the arrival of Antonio Valencia as soon as the transfer window opened.

The former Wigan Athletic man became the first Ecuadorian to play for United, and was quickly tipped for big things by Sir Alex. "Antonio is a player we have admired for some time now, having spent the last two years in the Premier League with Wigan," said the United manager. "I am sure his pace and ability will make a significant contribution to the team."

Antonio, who cut short his holiday to sign on the dotted line with the Reds, outlined how much the move meant to him. "Joining Manchester United is a dream come true for me. I have enjoyed my time at Wigan, but I am thrilled to have the chance to challenge for the biggest honours in club football here. Playing in front of 76,000 fans alongside players like Wayne Rooney, Rio Ferdinand and Ryan Giggs will be an amazing experience."

**Name:** Antonio Valencia
**Position:** Winger
**Born:** 4 August 1985, Lago Agrio, Ecuador
**Previous Clubs:** El Nacional, Villarreal, Wigan Athletic

# Adem Ljajic

Serbian starlet Adem Ljajic actually joined United midway through the 2008/09 season, but was immediately loaned back to previous club Partizan Belgrade to further his education. Adem has since returned to Carrington to train with his future United colleagues, and the young attacking midfielder, who will officially become a Red in January 2010, is already setting his sights high. "The quality is very high over here because you're training with great players," he says. "Working with these top players can only help me improve. Training with the team has allowed me to see how things work so I know what to expect when I come here. And I hope that when I join I will be involved with the first team from the start."

**Name:** Adem Ljajic
**Position:** Attacking midfielder
**Born:** 29 September 1991, Novi Pazar, Serbia
**Previous Clubs:** Partizan Belgrade

# Gabriel Obertan

Tipped as one of the most promising young talents to emerge from French football in recent years, versatile forward Gabriel Obertan can play in a variety of attacking positions. The France under-21 international possesses pace in abundance, as well as a great array of trickery. He burst onto the first team scene at Bordeaux aged just 17, before being loaned to L'Orient to gain more regular action last season. His move to United surprised many, including the player himself, but Sir Alex Ferguson has confidence in the youngster, saying: "Gabriel is a player we have tracked for a few years, and is an exciting prospect. We like to get young players and develop them, and we will see that in Gabriel over the next two years."

**Name:** Gabriel Obertan
**Position:** Winger
**Born:** 26 February 1989, Pantin, France
**Previous Clubs:** Paris-Saint Germain, Lorient (loan), Bordeaux

# Strike a pose for the 2009/10 team photo

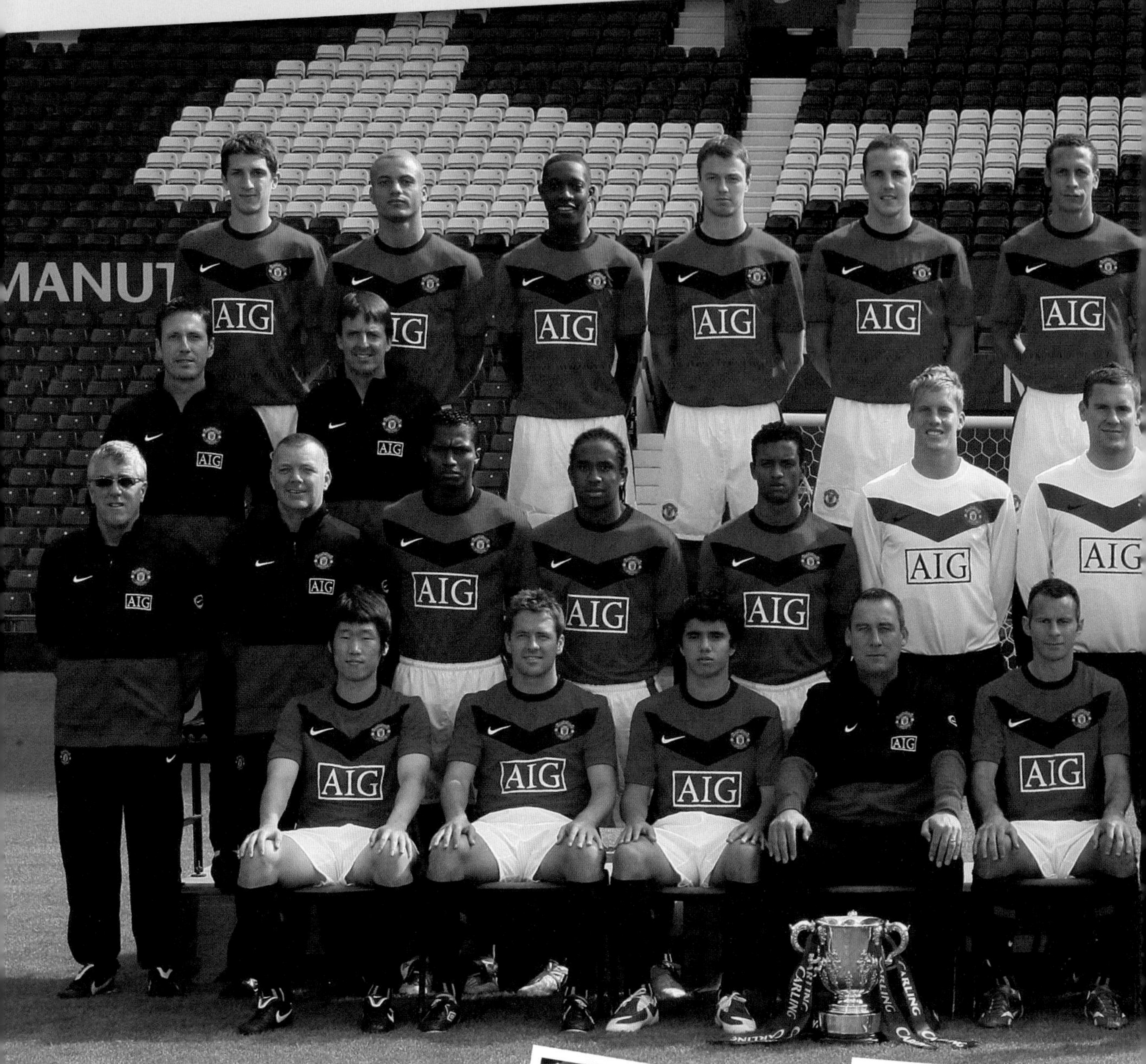


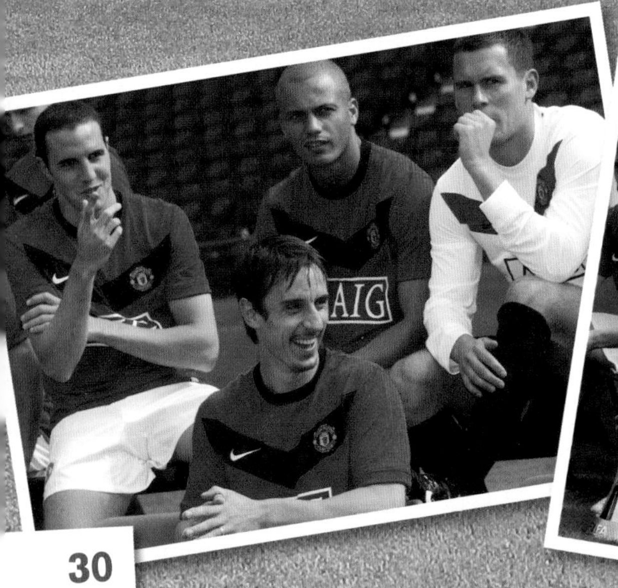


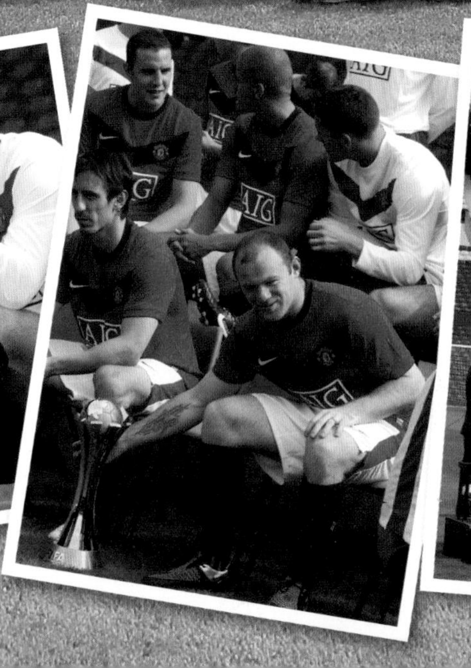


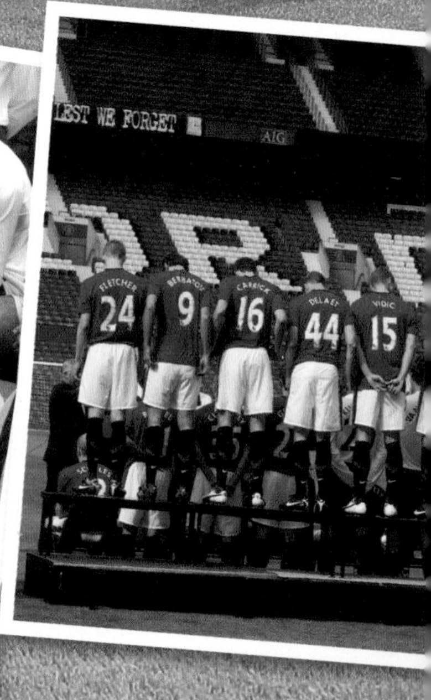

# Top 10 2008/09 Goals

The Reds' 2008/09 campaign was memorable not only for the trophies, but for some quite sensational goals scored during the course of the season. Here's our top 10...

## 10. Wayne Rooney v Blackburn Rovers (a), 4 October 2008, Premier League

The short trip to Ewood Park is always tricky, but United made light work of Rovers on this occasion. Wes Brown opened the scoring before a superb second from Rooney. Ronaldo out-muscled his marker, raced into the area and pulled a cross back for Wazza, who hammered a first-time shot into the top corner to make sure of three well-earned points.

## 9. Rafael da Silva v Arsenal (a), 8 November 2008, Premier League

It was too little, too late in terms of taking any points home from the Emirates Stadium, but Rafael's goal confirmed the young Brazilian's phenomenal potential. Not only can he defend and bomb forward with great gusto, but the little teenager can also control a clearance perfectly and lash a superb 18-yard volley into the bottom corner - with his wrong foot, no less.

## 8. Carlos Tevez v Manchester City (h), 10 May 2009, Premier League

The Argentine striker often reserved his goals for the most important situations, and this crucial end of season win over Manchester City was a great example. Exquisite control from Dimitar Berbatov allowed Tevez the chance to face Richard Dunne, shift the ball past him and rocket a shot inside Shay Given's post. A fine way to bag his final goal at Old Trafford as a United player.

## 7. Darron Gibson v Hull City (a), 24 May 2009, Premier League

The Premier League title was done and dusted, while the Champions League final loomed large, giving a number of the Reds' fringe players an outing at the KC Stadium. Gibbo was one who took his opportunity in style, scoring a stunning winner. The young midfielder received the ball 35 yards out, took aim from the left edge of the area and hammered a superb shot into Boaz Myhill's top left-hand corner.

## 6. Danny Welbeck v Stoke City (h), 15 November 2008, Premier League

Teenage striker Danny Welbeck had been building a promising reputation for himself in the United youth teams and Reserves, before he burst into first team football with a stunning Premier League debut goal against Stoke. Having swapped passes with Manucho and advanced on goal, the Longsight-born striker arrowed an unstoppab[le] shot in from 30 yards, via the underside of the crossbar, to give the surest sign yet that he can handle senior football.

## 5. Cristiano Ronaldo v Blackburn Rovers (h), 21 February 2009, Premier League

With Ronaldo at Old Trafford, there were never any queues to take the free-kicks. He was the man for the job, and it's hard to argue when he could thump home efforts like this one. With United out of sorts and level against Rovers, he was fouled on the corner of the visitors' area at the Stretford End. Despite the tight angle and a towering wall to negotiate, Ronaldo hammered a stunning effort into the far top corner.

## 4. Ryan Giggs v West Ham (a), 8 February 2009, Premier League

He's more of a central midfielder nowadays, but Ryan Giggs relished a rare return to left-wing duties against West Ham, as he scored a priceless winner at Upton Park. The veteran star twice shaped to cross, selling spectacular dummies to two Hammers defenders before drilling a low right-footed shot through a crowd of players and past England goalkeeper Robert Green.

## 3. Cristiano Ronaldo v Arsenal (a), 5 May 2009, Champions League semi-final

Arsenal were gamely battling for a route back into the Champions League semi-final, despite trailing by three goals. This left United with space to exploit, and did they ever, in the most clinical fashion. Vidic heads clear, Ronaldo backheels to Park and starts sprinting, Park feeds Rooney, Rooney squares and there, some 10 seconds after his previous touch, is Ronaldo again to hammer home. Knife. Through. Butter.

## 2. Cristiano Ronaldo v Porto (a), 15 April 2009, Champions League quarter-final

Ronaldo scored some phenomenal goals during his six-year United career, but this was arguably the finest of the lot. Taking a pass from Anderson just inside the hosts' half, the winger took a touch and immediately smashed a right-foot shot which hurtled straight into the top corner from some 40 yards, and took United through to the Champions League semi-finals. Breathtakingly simple, but utterly unstoppable.

## 1. Federico Macheda v Aston Villa (h), 5 April 2009, Premier League

It's the circumstances as much as the breathtaking skill which makes this United's goal of the season. The Reds were desperate for a win, after two straight defeats, and were level against Villa as injury-time began. Then, up stepped 17-year-old debutant Kiko Macheda, who controlled Ryan Giggs' pass and turned Luke Young in a single swivel, before curling home an incredible winner. It pretty much confirmed United as champions, and assured Kiko of a place in Reds folklore.

# Wayne's World

## Relive the Club World Cup triumph through the eyes of Wayne Rooney

United made history in December 2008 when they became the first British club to win the FIFA Club World Cup. Wayne Rooney was at his clinical best during the tournament in Japan, coming off the bench to score twice in the semi-final victory over Gamba Osaka, before firing the winner against Liga de Quito in the final to crown United champions of the world...

## December 2008

### 15 Monday

This was my third trip to Japan with United and it's somewhere I always enjoy visiting. The support for the club out there is amazing – there were hundreds of fans at the airport and hotel in Yokohama to greet us when we arrived. We wanted to do our best to entertain them and put on a good show and, of course, come back with the trophy.

### 16 Tuesday

A lot of the lads were still adjusting to the time difference and getting over the long flight from the UK. Some really struggled with sleeping but I wasn't short of sleep – I can sleep anywhere! I managed to get around eight hours on the plane so I didn't feel too bad, but it still takes a bit of time to acclimatise. I think the fact that it wasn't boiling hot like it usually is when we come to Asia on pre-season tours helped – it wasn't as cold as Manchester, but it wasn't far off!

### 17 Wednesday

We continued our preparations for Thursday's semi-final against Gamba Osaka and trained at Yokohama Stadium for the first time. We knew it wouldn't be an easy match – I'd played two pre-season games against Urawa Reds, who, like Gamba, are in the J-League, and they were tough opponents. So we knew we needed to stay focused and make sure we concentrated for the full 90 minutes.

## 18 Thursday

Matchday v Gamba Osaka

It was a great feeling to make it into Sunday's final and I was really happy with my two goals; Vida, Ronaldo and Fletch also got on the score-sheet and overall it was a good win. You don't get many chances to become world champions and we all felt that winning the tournament could really spur us on for the second half of the season and send out a powerful message to the rest of the Premier League. During the Osaka game I heard our fans singing 'Champions of England, Champions of Europe' and I remember thinking it would be great if they can add 'Champions of the World' to that.

## 19 Friday

After training we all went for a stroll in the sun around Yokohama harbour which was a few minutes walk from the hotel. Between training and games there is always quite a lot of time to kill on these trips. I spent most of my free time either watching DVDs, listening to my iPod or playing pool in the hotel games room.

## 20 Saturday

We had our last training session in Japan ahead of Sunday's final. It's always been an ambition of mine to have the complete set of winners' medals in my trophy cabinet. I already had Champions League, Premier League, Carling Cup and Community Shield ones, and I desperately wanted to add the Club World Cup to those.

Matchday v Liga de Quito

## 21 Sunday

It was a great feeling to be crowned world champions and I was really pleased to score the winner – scoring goals in consecutive games is great for your confidence and when you're confident you feel like every shot is going to go in. To win any award is an achievement in itself and I was delighted to be given the Player of the Tournament prize; it topped off a great week. We were disappointed to see Vida get sent off, but thankfully we still managed to win the game. Our main objective at the start of each season is to win every competition we're involved in and to have come home as world champions was a fantastic achievement and something we'll always be very proud of.

# Wayne's World

**MANCHESTER UNITED 5**
Vidic 28,
Ronaldo 45,
Rooney 75, 79
Fletcher 78.

**GAMBA OSAKA 3**
Yamazaki 74,
Endo 85 (pen),
Hashimoto 90

**MANCHESTER UNITED**
Van der Sar
Neville
Ferdinand
Vidic (Evans 69)
Evra
Nani
Anderson
Scholes (Fletcher 67)
Giggs
Ronaldo
Tevez (Rooney 73)

**Subs not used:**
Kuszczak
Amos
Rafael
O'Shea
Carrick
Gibson, Park
Welbeck

**Booked:**
Rooney

**GAMBA OSAKA**
Fujigaya
Nakazawa
Yamaguchi
Kaji
Hashimoto
Yasuda
Endo
Bando (Terada 85)
Myojin
Lucas
Yamazaki

**Subs not used:**
Matsuyo
Shimohira
Futagawa
Kurata
Takei
Roni

**Booked:**
Yamaguchi

| MANCHESTER UNITED 1 | LIGA DE QUITO 0 |
|---|---|
| Rooney 73 | |

## MANCHESTER UNITED
Van der Sar
Rafael (Neville 85)
Ferdinand
Vidic
Evra
Ronaldo
Carrick
Anderson (Fletcher 88)
Park
Tevez (Evans 51)
Rooney

**Subs not used:**
Kuszczak
Amos
Berbatov
Giggs
Nani
Scholes
Welbeck
O'Shea
Gibson

**Booked:**
Anderson

**Sent off:**
Vidic

## LIGA DE QUITO
Cevallos
N.Araujo
Calle (Ambrosi 77)
Campos
Calderon
Reasco (Larrea 82)
Urrutia
W.Araujo
Manso
Luis Bolanos (Navia 87)
Bieler

**Subs not used:**
Dominguez
Obregon
Delgado
E.Vaca
D.Vaca
Chango
Viteri

**Booked:**
Bieler
Campos
Cevallos
Calle
W.Araujo

# The Road to Wembley

## 23/09/08 – Round 3 – United 3 Middlesbrough 1

Goals from Cristiano Ronaldo, Ryan Giggs and Nani booked United's place in the Carling Cup fourth round, but the victory was marred by a horror tackle on Rodrigo Possebon. The Brazilian midfielder was carried off midway through the second half following a high challenge from Emanuel Pogatetz, who was dismissed for the shocking offence. Earlier, Ronaldo's 25th minute header had been cancelled out by substitute Adam Johnson's volley, but Giggs calmly put United ahead late on, before Nani slotted home a clincher in the fifth of nine added minutes.

**United:** Amos; Rafael, Brown, Vidic, O'Shea; Nani, Anderson, Possebon (Gibson 72), Giggs (Manucho 84); Welbeck, Ronaldo (Tevez 61).

"Old Trafford is a big stage, but the young lads did really well from start to finish." *Ryan Giggs*

"We kept the ball well and had a lot of chances even though the goal came late on." *Rodrigo Possebon*

## 11/11/08 – Round 4 – United 1 QPR 0

An impressive blend of maturity and patience, as well as a late Carlos Tevez penalty, helped the Reds overcome a dogged Queens Park Rangers side at Old Trafford. The visitors were largely effective in restricting United to long-range strikes in the first period with Tevez and Anderson going closest. QPR continued to offer little going forward after the break as the Reds upped the tempo. Nani flashed a wicked drive past Radek Cerny's right-hand post, while Park smacked the other with a powerful, rising effort. Anderson and Tevez were denied soon after, but there was no stopping the latter from the penalty spot on 76 minutes after substitute Danny Welbeck was upended in the box.

**United:** Kuszczak; Rafael, Neville (Vidic 89), Evans, O'Shea; Gibson, Possebon (Welbeck 72), Anderson; Nani, Tevez, Park.

## 03/12/08 – Quarter-final – United 5 Blackburn 3

A Carlos Tevez quadruple sealed an impressive victory over Paul Ince's men to send the Reds into the last four. The Argentine claimed the opener on 36 minutes when a combination of he and Aaron Mokoena dived to meet Ryan Giggs' in-swinging free-kick and send the ball into the net. Four minutes later, Nani struck a second after a neat one-two with Tevez. Benni McCarthy handed Blackburn a lifeline after the break, but United hit back through Tevez's penalty conversion and a simple side-foot finish which completed his hat-trick. It looked like being a nervy final few minutes when Matt Derbyshire and McCarthy fired two late goals for the visitors, but Tevez wrapped things up in injury time with a brilliant low, dipping volley past Paul Robinson.

**United:** Foster; Rafael, Neville, Evans, O'Shea (Evra 66); Nani, Gibson, Possebon (Scholes 66); Anderson, Giggs (Manucho 71), Tevez.

"It's the first time I've scored four in a game in my career and I'm very proud to have achieved this in a United shirt." *Carlos Tevez*

## 07/01/09 – Semi-final 1 – Derby 1 United 0

United endured an uncomfortable evening at Pride Park and lost out to a fine first-half strike from the impressive Kris Commons. With new manager Nigel Clough watching from the stands, Derby set about their task with a real energy and endeavour which had a significant effect on United's rhythm throughout the 90 minutes. It was all Derby for the majority of the opening period, and they deservedly took the lead on the half-hour mark when the unopposed Commons let fly from 25 yards with an unstoppable left-foot rocket. United continued to struggle to get out of first gear after the re-start and in the end were relieved to see Commons, Hulse and Green all fail to extend the Rams' first leg advantage.

**United:** Kuszczak; Rafael, Vidic, Evans, O'Shea; Anderson (Carrick 74), Scholes (Ronaldo 63), Gibson, Nani; Tevez, Welbeck (Rooney 63).

"We knew we were going to have to battle hard, but I don't think we did it well enough all over the pitch and they certainly did better than us in that area." *Jonny Evans*

## 20/01/09 – Semi-final 2 – United 4 Derby 2, agg 4-3

It was a bittersweet evening for the Reds after they booked a Carling Cup final place at Wembley despite an epidemic of injuries. Rafael, Gary Neville, Ryan Giggs, Jonny Evans, Nani and Anderson - who was carried off on a stretcher - all picked up knocks as United battled their way to victory. Commons went close to scoring his second of the tie with a swerved effort on six minutes, but ten minutes later the Reds were level on aggregate thanks to Nani's fine strike. O'Shea slotted home soon after, before Tevez headed a third. Barnes gave Derby hope ten minutes from time when he converted from the spot, but United responded in kind through Ronaldo's 89th-minute penalty. Barnes curled home an injury-time free-kick, but it was too little too late – the Reds were off to Wembley.

**United:** Foster; Rafael (Fletcher 42), Neville (Chester 67), Evans, O'Shea; Giggs (Ronaldo 58), Gibson, Anderson, Nani; Welbeck, Tevez.

"We knew we had to be offensive from the start and scoring two early goals was a big boost. We deserved to win and everyone is buzzing about going to Wembley." *Darron Gibson*

# Carling Cup Final

## Cup final hero and Man of the Match Ben Foster looks back on a memorable day at Wembley...

"I remember being really excited in the lead-up to the final and thinking to myself, not only is this a great opportunity to win a medal, it's a chance for me to remind people what I'm all about.

"When I finished my loan spell at Watford [in May 2007] I had a little bit of a reputation as a decent up-and-coming goalkeeper, but I had an absolute nightmare with injuries when I came back to United and missed a lot of football. Things gradually started to improve for me and knowing I was in contention to play in a cup final for the biggest club in the world was a great feeling - it had been heartbreaking to watch United win things when I couldn't be involved.

"I was over the moon when the gaffer told me I was starting. He was very brave with his team selection on the day, he could have just picked the 'usuals' and probably made it an easier game for us, but he kept faith with the young lads yet again. I always go out and try to be confident with the things I feel I'm best at and I was pleased with my overall performance, especially as I hadn't actually played many games up to that point in the season.

"I didn't feel particularly nervous when it went to penalties – there isn't really too much pressure on goalkeepers in that situation, it's on the player taking the spot-kick because they're expected to score. As a keeper, you've just got to stand there and hope you guess the right way. Thankfully I managed to do that with O'Hara's penalty, before Bentley struck his wide.

"A lot was made of the research I did just before the shoot-out with our goalkeeping coach Eric Steele and Edwin [van der Sar] who wasn't involved in the game, but was watching from the sidelines. Eric had a video of some of Tottenham's recent penalties on an iPod, including one from O'Hara. The use of the iPod was a new innovation Eric brought to the club when he joined and it was a great tool to have at that point. Both Eric and Edwin told me to be as intimidating as possible and stand up for as long as I could and thankfully things worked out great for me.

"Of course, the win wasn't just down to me; our lads were fantastic with their penalties and put them away with real conviction. It was a great feeling to lift the trophy afterwards and have that winners' medal round my neck - I hope it's the first of many to come in the future."

## The Teams

### MANCHESTER UNITED

Foster; O'Shea (Vidic 76), Ferdinand, Evans, Evra; Ronaldo, Scholes, Gibson (Giggs 91), Nani; Tevez, Welbeck (Anderson 56).

**Subs not used:**
Kuszczak, Park, Possebon, Eckersley.

**Booked:**
O'Shea, Ronaldo, Scholes

### TOTTENHAM HOTSPUR

Gomes; Corluka, Dawson, King, Assou-Ekotto; Lennon (Bentley 102), Jenas (Bale 98), Zokora, Modric; Bent, Pavlyuchenko (O'Hara 65).

**Subs not used:**
Alnwick, Huddlestone, Gunter, Taarabt.

## COACH'S VIEW

### Assistant manager, Mike Phelan

"The Carling Cup run and the way we progressed through the competition was important for the club from a development point of view. We introduced numerous young players who grew throughout the tournament and improved many different aspects of their game. They saw the progression they could make through the competition and the opportunity that was there for them and I think they all enjoyed the ride. It's part and parcel of the history at this club that young players get their opportunity to play in big games and the fact that they did that and ended up winning the trophy enabled them to pick up valuable experience and will encourage them to want more."

# The Star Makers

**United's continued success is built on a foundation of nurturing and developing top young players...**

The 2008/09 season provided glaring proof of United's reliance on the development of youth. While Sir Alex Ferguson's side continued to feature veteran stalwarts Ryan Giggs, Paul Scholes and Gary Neville, opportunities were handed to a glut of burgeoning young talents – almost all home-grown and developed within the club's Academy over a number of years.

Ever since the days of the Busby Babes, United have put tremendous faith in creating superstars rather than buying them. Indeed, all of the club's top five appearance-makers (Giggs, Sir Bobby Charlton, Bill Foulkes, Scholes and Neville) came through the Reds' youth ranks. That's why, when the club's Carrington training ground was opened, it was flanked by an £8million building exclusively dedicated to the club's Academy.

It is there and in the main offices at Carrington where the club's future is carefully groomed and shaped on a daily basis, by a team headed by Academy Director Brian McClair. Prohibitive Premier League rules on the recruitment of young talents means United now have to cast a wider net in order to snare the best budding players.

That's why the likes of Italian striker Kiko Macheda, who joined from Lazio in 2007, are becoming an increasingly integral part of the United youth set-up. Wherever the talent comes from, however, the story remains the same: the finest players will catch the eye, join the club and quickly ascend through the ranks before reaching the cusp of the first team.

Firstly, dependent on the age at which they join the Reds, players must rise through the club's various teams, which range from the under-9s to the under-18s. After graduating from a three-year scholarship between the ages of 16 and 18, the boys are either taken on professional forms or released to forge careers at other clubs.

The vast majority of those taken on spend their playing time in the Reserves, under the tutelage of manager Ole Gunnar Solskjaer and his assistant, Warren Joyce. "We just try to create good habits for the lads," says former United striker Solskjaer. "If they come out of our team being professional and knowing what it takes to make a good professional, then they've got a decent chance of making it in football.

"They've got all the talent in the world, no problem, but being a good professional is something we strive for every day. We want them to reach their maximum every day and we make sure they play the right way - the Manchester United way. If they do that to a good level with us, then they can be ready for that step up whenever they might be required by Sir Alex."

# Ones To Watch

United's youth and Reserve teams are brimming with talented youngsters. Here are five who are hoping to make waves in the near future...

## Robert Brady ⇨

**Born: 14 January 1992; Dublin, Ireland**
**Position: Winger**

Robbie arrived at United in July 2008 as a highly-rated young winger, and his first season with the Reds' U18s did little to dampen the expectation surrounding him. Regarded as one of the best young talents to emerge from Irish football in recent years, Brady is an extremely quick, tricky left-sided player who can also ply his trade in the centre of the park or at left-back. With his slaloming runs and deadly set-pieces, Robbie is able to create and score goals in equal measure, and he is the kind of traditional winger which has so often succeeded at United.

## ⇦ Matthew James

**Born: 22 July 1991; Bacup, England**
**Position: Midfielder**

Matt was another player who earned himself a professional contract at the start of the 2009/10 season, after catching the eye for the under-18s and Reserves. The Rochdale-born youngster enjoyed an impressive 2008/09 campaign with the Reds' second-string, taking great strides in his all-round game and also improving his goals return. Matt is versatile enough to fill in as a defender when required, but is best used in the centre of midfield, where he can demonstrate his excellent array of passing over short or long distances, as well as his missile-like shooting with either foot.

# Davide Petrucci

→

**Born: 5 October 1991; Rome, Italy**
**Position: Attacking midfielder**

It says much for the quick adaptation of the Italian that, within half a season of arriving at United, he had been handed a first-team squad number. The gifted young playmaker caught the eye during a prolific 2007/08 campaign in the Roma youth ranks, and he was quickly snapped up by the Reds. He continued to impress with a string of fine displays for United's under-18s during 2008/09, and also stood out in a handful of appearances for the Reserves, before injury cut his season short. His passing, shooting and runs are outstanding, while he is menacingly accurate from set-pieces anywhere near the opposition area.

# Scott Wootton

←

**Born: 12 September 1991; Birkenhead, England**
**Position: Central defender**

Having joined from rivals Liverpool, the tough-tackling defender quickly set about making a name for himself with United's youth team. The Birkenhead-born youngster is notable for his mature decision-making on the field and his reading of the game – two key attributes for any budding centre-back. Scott is a very vocal member of Paul McGuinness' under-18s, and his leadership qualities have surfaced as his career has evolved. Sir Alex Ferguson demonstrated his admiration for Wootton in the summer of 2009, when he signed the youngster up on professional forms.

# Corry Evans

→

**Born: 30 July 1990; Belfast, Northern Ireland**
**Position: Defensive midfielder / defender**

While Jonny Evans was seamlessly integrating into the United first team during the 2008/09 campaign, his younger brother, Corry, was making strides of his own through the Reds' ranks. The combative youngster, who began as a central midfielder but can operate almost anywhere in midfield or defence, shone in the Reserves under Ole Gunnar Solskjaer and earned himself a nomination for the Reserves Player of the Year award. As well as his defensive tenacity and midfield playmaking, Corry has also shown that he has an eye for goal, and is fast developing into a fine all-rounder.

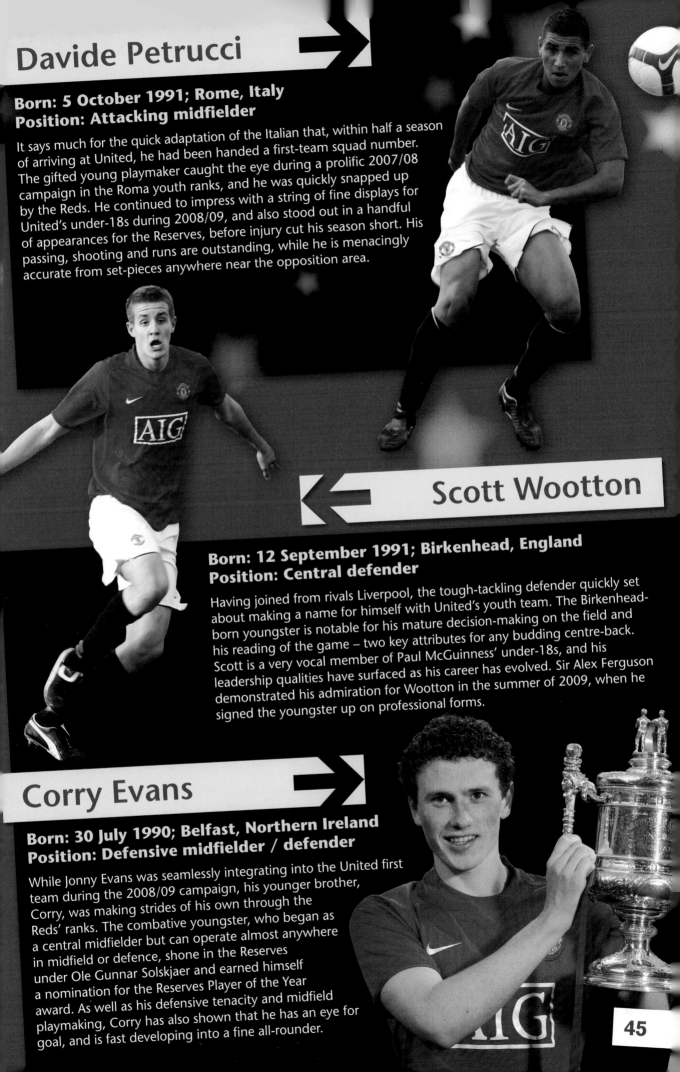

# Carrington Confidential

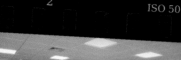

### → First team dressing room

The players returned to a new home on arrival back at Carrington in the summer of 2007. Following a full refurbishment, the Reds' new-look first team dressing room was extended with an extra area for physio treatment also erected.

### → The boot room

Kit manager Albert Morgan is responsible for ensuring the players are aptly suited and booted for training and matchday. He works out of two boot rooms, both of which are in close proximity to the first team dressing room. One even has a state-of-the-art boot dryer to dry out the players' footwear on those (frequently) rainy days.

### → MUTV studio

Formed in 1998, MUTV has grown substantially both in terms of its size and subscription figures and is now broadcast in over forty countries. The channel's reporters regularly interview members of the senior squad at their Carrington-based studio which features state-of-the-art lighting, recording and editing equipment.

Opened in January 2000, the Reds' state-of-the-art Carrington training complex is the nerve centre of the club, a place fans very rarely get to see. An initial £14million outlay on the main building was followed by a further £8million investment two years later in the Academy building, situated opposite. Twelve outdoor pitches (two of which have undersoil heating), first class training and rehabilitation equipment, plush changing facilities and a sprawling canteen are just some of the centre's features. Here, we take you on a behind-the-scenes tour...

## → The gym

The players are put through their paces by strength and conditioning coach Mike Clegg during sessions in the gym, which is housed on the ground floor. A cardiovascular and weights section with free weights and resistance machinery are all on offer, as are balance training machines and spinning bikes, on which the players warm-up before training.

## → The pool area

Carrington's 25-metre indoor swimming pool, Jacuzzi, hydrotherapy pool, steam room and sauna offer the players a variety of relaxation options after training. The pool itself is often used to aid recovery from injury, as is the unique water treadmill, which the club had installed during the 2006/07 season.

## THE ACADEMY

Standing opposite the main building is the club's Academy facility which was officially opened by Sir Alex Ferguson and Sir Bobby Charlton. Split over two levels, the building is adorned throughout with visual reminders of the players who have worn the well-trodden path through United's ranks.

The ground floor comprises 12 dressing rooms (one for match officials), as well as a full-size indoor artificial pitch. Aside from being used for football activity - the first team will, during times of inclement weather, train there - the pitch is often the setting for various commercial events such as kit photo-shoots and interviews. It is also used by Manchester United Soccer Schools and other club departments who hold one-off football clinics.

On most evenings, the facilities – which also include a full-size outdoor artificial pitch - are used by the club's youth teams. High above the pitch is a balcony from which proud parents can watch on. Also on the first floor is a classroom, which is used for educational sessions with United's young scholars, as well as a main reception room which is the location for Sir Alex's weekly press conference.

## → The canteen

Based on the first floor, the canteen seats around 100 and is used by all club employees based at Carrington, including Sir Alex, coaching staff, first team, Reserves and Academy players, as well as all operational staff. Lunch is served between 12 and 2pm, with snacks and drinks available all the day. The man responsible for deciding on the culinary delights on offer is club dietician Trevor Lea.

47

# Practice makes perfect

as the players train under
Sir Alex's watchful eye

# My Favourite Things

## Just what do the players enjoy away from the pitch?

## John O'Shea

Favourite music: I like most kinds but particular favourites are indie and rock.
Favourite band: Snow Patrol
Favourite TV programme: 24
Favourite film: The Godfather Part 2
Favourite actor: Robert De Niro
How do you relax away from football? Walking my dog or playing golf.
Favourite food: Chinese
Favourite pre-match meal: Pasta and chicken
Favourite non-football sporting hero: Tiger Woods
Favourite footballing hero: Paul McGrath
Favourite subject at school: Economics
Favourite holiday destination: Barbados or Dubai
If you could have any superpower, what would it be? I'd like to be invisible.
If you were stranded on a desert island, what would you want to have with you?
My mobile phone, my DVD player and the 24 box-set.
If you weren't a footballer what would you be? I would have gone to University
in Ireland and done a business studies or economics degree.

## Ryan Giggs

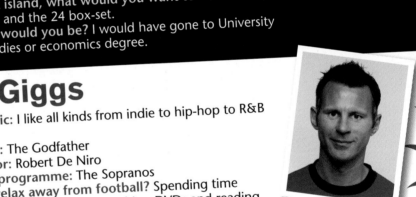

Favourite music: I like all kinds from indie to hip-hop to R&B
- everything!
Favourite film: The Godfather
Favourite actor: Robert De Niro
Favourite TV programme: The Sopranos
How do you relax away from football? Spending time
with my children, playing golf, watching DVDs and reading.
Favourite holiday destination: Portugal
If you could have any superpower, what would it be? I'd like to be
invisible so I could spy on people!
If you were stranded on a desert island, what would you want to have with you?
My family.
If you weren't a footballer what would you be? Maybe a rugby league player.
Favourite subject at school: I wasn't a big fan of school! But if I had to pick one then
I'd say Geography.

## Wayne Rooney

Favourite music: Rock.
Favourite band: Stereophonics
Favourite actor: Brad Pitt
Favourite TV programme: I love watching Coronation
Street and EastEnders but I'd have to say Shameless.
Favourite holiday destination: Barbados
If you could have any superpower, what would it be?
To be able to fly over traffic when I'm stuck in it!
If you weren't a footballer what would you be? I don't
know, I'd probably be working with my dad.

# Michael Carrick

Favourite music: R&B and hip-hop.
Favourite film: The Game
Favourite actor: Robert De Niro
Favourite TV programme: 24
Favourite subject at school: Geography
How do you relax away from football? Watching TV, playing on the PSP.
Favourite holiday destination: Dubai
If you could have any superpower, what would it be? I'd like to be a super healer so I could make people healthy.
If you were stranded on a desert island, what would you want to have with you? The missus!
If you weren't a footballer what would you be? I'd probably still be doing something in sport, maybe a football coach.

# Rio Ferdinand

Favourite music: Old soul, reggae, R&B and pop - a bit of everything.
Favourite film: Silence of the Lambs
Favourite actor: Robert De Niro
Favourite TV programme: EastEnders
Favourite subject at school: PE and drama
How do you relax away from football? Watching soaps
Favourite holiday destination: Cannes
If you could have any superpower, what would it be? I'd like to be invisible.
If you were stranded on a desert island, what would you want to have with you? Other than family, I'd take my iPod.
If you weren't a footballer what would you be? I'd probably be working with kids in the local community.

# Darren Fletcher

Favourite film: Shawshank Redemption
Favourite TV programme: Prison Break
Favourite actor: Tom Hanks because he always puts in a classic performance.
Favourite comedian: Lee Evans
Favourite musician: Notorious B.I.G
Favourite food: Haggis and potatoes
Favourite drink: Orange Lucozade
Favourite pizza topping: Plain cheese
Non-football sporting hero: Muhammed Ali
Favourite pre-match meal: Chicken and spaghetti with ketchup on top.
Footballing hero: Fernando Redondo
If you weren't a footballer what would you be? A PE teacher
If you could have any superpower, what would it be? To be able to fly.
Favourite holiday destination: New York

51

# 100 Years of Old Trafford

**A Century at the Theatre:** February 2010 will mark 100 years since the opening of Old Trafford. United's home ground has played witness to some of the most memorable occasions in the history of football, and the Reds' rich past in particular. Here are some of the landmark moments in the story of Old Trafford...

**1910** – Designed by Archibald Leith, built by Messrs Brameld and Smith of Manchester and bankrolled by United chairman John Henry (to the tune of £60,000), Old Trafford hosted its first game: United vs Liverpool. The Reds couldn't conjure up a fitting result as the visitors won 4-3, but the true spectacle was the venue, labelled by The Sporting Chronicle as: "An honour to Manchester and the home of a team who can do wonders when they are so disposed."

**1915** – With the construction of Wembley still eight years away, the FA Cup Final was held at grounds across the country. Old Trafford staged the 1911 replay between Bradford City and Newcastle United, before hosting the 1915 Final proper when Sheffield United secured a 3-0 win over Chelsea.

**1920** – In December, Old Trafford hosted its largest pre-Second World War attendance. 70,504 spectators crammed in to watch the Reds take on Aston Villa, but left disappointed as the midlanders ran out 3-1 winners. The ground's all-time record attendance actually came in 1939, when 76,962 supporters witnessed an FA Cup semi-final between Wolverhampton Wanderers and Grimsby Town.

**1941** – After five years of extensive roofing, the stadium was virtually destroyed by German bombs during the Second World War. The War Damage Commission allocated just over £22,000 to clear and rebuild the stadium, while Manchester City offered to host United's home games at Maine Road – at a cost of £5,000 per season and a percentage of the gate.

**1949** – A game at last! A decade after the last match in M16 – due to the war and its subsequent bombing – Bolton Wanderers visited Old Trafford and were trounced 3-0.

**1957** – By now fully restored and roofed on all sides, Old Trafford played host to its first match under floodlights. It was Bolton who shone in the spotlight, however, running out 2-0 winners.

**1965** – The ground's obstructive roof pillars were replaced by cantilevering and the United Road stand was extended to hold 20,000 spectators, while English football's first private boxes were introduced. This was in the run-up to England's hosting of the 1966 World Cup, in which Old Trafford staged three group games.

# The Kit

## Inspired by history

United's home and away kits for the 2009/10 season have been specially designed to mark the Old Trafford anniversary.

Each feature a special commemorative tag at the side of the shirt and large chevron across the chest, reflecting the design of the shirts worn by the Reds when the team won its first FA Cup in 1909.

The home kit is made up of the traditional red shirt, featuring a black chevron, along with white shorts and black socks, while the away attire consists of a black shirt with a blue chevron, black shorts and black socks.

Rio Ferdinand says the players are always excited by the new kits and insists the historical aspect of the latest designs act as an inspiration to everyone.

"Maintaining the traditions of the club is very important," declares the defender. "Last season we had the blue kit to remember the European Cup winners of 1968 and these date back to the 1900s to celebrate 100 years of Old Trafford. This club has always taken pride in its history - it acts as an inspiration to all of us and it's great to see it represented in the new kits."

Ji-sung Park echoes those sentiments, adding: "It always feels great to put the kit on and there is always a great meaning behind our kits. I really like the chevron feature – I like to think of it as 'V' for victory."

### Then...

### ...Now

**1990** – In the aftermath of the Hillsborough disaster and the subsequent Taylor Report, the Government insisted that all stadia in England become all-seater. That meant Old Trafford's attendance fell to an all-time low of 44,000.

**1995** – United extended the North Stand to three tiers, taking the capacity up to 55,000. Within five years, both the West Stand (Stretford End) and East Stand (Scoreboard End) were given second tiers, adding another 13,000 seats. The reward for Old Trafford's ongoing facelift, which made it England's only 5-star stadium under UEFA's ratings system, was to host the 2002/03 Champions League final between AC Milan and Juventus.

**2005** – The expansion continued, with another 8,000 seats shoehorned into the North-East and North-West quadrants, while the stadium's hospitality continued to set the standards with yet another stylish makeover. Old Trafford's record attendance for a United game rose to 76,098 when the Reds hammered Blackburn Rovers 4-1.

**2009** – Old Trafford remains English football's biggest club stadium, with an average gate of 75,304 during the 2008/09 season – and a grand total of almost 1.5 million spectators over the course of the campaign.

# Did You Know?

1. United haven't always been United. Originally, the club was formed by workers on the Lancashire and Yorkshire Railway depot in 1878, under the name of Newton Heath L&YR FC. Latterly the name was simplified to Newton Heath before, in 1902, it was changed to Manchester United.

2. To put Cristiano Ronaldo's £80 million move to Real Madrid into perspective; the club's first ever transfer, which brought Gilbert Godsmark from Ashford in 1900, cost a whopping £40.

3. Former United manager Sir Matt Busby is perhaps the most important figure in the club's history, but the Scot spent the vast majority of his playing career with two of the Reds' bitterest rivals – Manchester City and Liverpool.

4. When the Reds first won the European Cup in 1968, the squad contained three winners of the Ballon d'Or (otherwise known as the European Footballer of the Year award) – Denis Law, Sir Bobby Charlton and George Best.

5. Sir Alex Ferguson's influence isn't just confined to football, he's also impacted on the dictionary. In 2005, the Collins English Dictionary included the manager's phrase 'squeaky bum time', which he used to describe the nerves of the 2002/03 title race.

6. Ryan Giggs is the only player to have scored in every Premier League season since the competition began in 1992 – that's 17 consecutive campaigns!

7. Last season's Champions League final defeat in Rome was the first time the Reds have failed to win a major European competition final, having won all four previous finals (three in the European Cup / Champions League, one in the European Cup Winners' Cup).

8. In the league table comprising every Premier League season since the competition's inception in 1992, United started the 2009/10 season with a lead of 173 points over second-placed Arsenal. The top five is made up by Chelsea, Liverpool and Aston Villa.

54

## Honours

FIFA Club World Cup (1): 2008

Intercontinental Cup (1): 1999

European Cup / UEFA Champions League (3): 1968, 1999, 2008

UEFA Cup Winners' Cup (1): 1991

European Super Cup (1): 1991

First Division / Premier League (18): 1907/08, 1910/11, 1951/52, 1955/56, 1956/57, 1964/65, 1966/67, 1992/93, 1993/94, 1995/96, 1996/97, 1998/99, 1999/2000, 2000/01, 2002/03, 2006/07, 2007/08, 2008/09

Second Division (2): 1935/36, 1974/75

FA Cup (11): 1909, 1948, 1963, 1977, 1983, 1985, 1990, 1994, 1996, 1999, 2004

League Cup (3): 1992, 2006, 2009

FA Charity/Community Shield (17 – 13 outright, 4 shared): 1908, 1911, 1952, 1956,1957, 1965*, 1967*, 1977*, 1983, 1990*, 1993, 1994, 1996, 1997, 2003, 2007, 2008 *shared

## Club Records*

*All stats correct up to 16 August, 2009.

### Top 5 appearance-makers

| | |
|---|---|
| Ryan Giggs | 806 |
| Sir Bobby Charlton | 758 |
| Bill Foulkes | 688 |
| Paul Scholes | 605 |
| Gary Neville | 570 |

### Top 5 goalscorers

| | |
|---|---|
| Sir Bobby Charlton | 249 |
| Denis Law | 237 |
| Jack Rowley | 211 |
| George Best | 179 |
| Dennis Viollet | 179 |

Most goals in a season (all competitions): Denis Law – 46 goals (1963/64)

Most team honours won: Ryan Giggs (30 – 11 League titles, 2 Champions Leagues, 4 FA Cups, 1 Club World Cup, 1 Intercontinental Cup, 1 UEFA Super Cup, 3 League Cups, 7 Charity / Community Shields)

Youngest first-team player: David Gaskell, 16 years 19 days (against Manchester City, Charity Shield, 24 October 1956)

Oldest first-team player: Billy Meredith, 46 years 281 days (against Derby County, First Division, 7 May 1921)

Biggest win: 10–0 v Anderlecht, European Cup Preliminary Round, second leg, 26 September 1956

Biggest defeats: 7-0 v Blackburn Rovers, First Division, 10 April 1926; v Aston Villa, First Division, 27 December 1930; v Wolverhampton Wanderers, Second Division, 26 December 1931

# Wordsearch

The United players can pick out a team-mate on a crowded pitch, but do you have the same vision? See if you can find the surnames of 10 Reds which are hidden in this wordsearch…

```
A  I  C  N  E  L  A  V  N  L
D  D  N  P  M  R  K  K  E  F
N  I  E  C  G  L  R  A  F  F
A  N  P  H  R  I  F  M  L  P
N  A  A  L  C  A  G  E  P  N
I  N  R  M  R  A  T  G  M  Q
D  C  K  N  L  C  M  J  S  Z
R  R  W  K  H  X  W  M  T  X
E  N  V  E  Y  E  N  O  O  R
F  B  R  L  E  V  A  N  S  K
```

Answers on Page 62

# Guess The Red

We blurred these photographs of three United stars.
Can you guess who they are? We've added clues to help you.

**Clue**

Always keep a cool head
in front of goal

**Clue**

This defender has the luck
of the Irish about him

**Clue**

His Korea has gone from strength
to strength at Old Trafford.

Answers on Page 62

# Anagrams

Unscramble the anagrams below to reveal the names
of 10 United players...

1. All Grey Vein

2. Rave Cat Ripe

3. Jam Divine Can

4. Bones Fret

5. Brews Won

6. Chow Alien Me

7. Snore Dan

8. He Calls Soup

9. Bravo Brad Tim Tie

10. Lick Chair Cream

Answers on Page 62

57

# Spot The Difference

**Can you spot the 7 differences between the two photographs?**

Answers on Page 62

# United Quiz

**Q1:** From which club did United sign Antonio Valencia?

**Q2:** Who manages the club's Reserve team?

**Q3:** What nationality is Nemanja Vidic?

**Q4:** In what year did United win the first Premier League title?

**Q5:** Who was the Reds' top scorer in the 2008/09 season?

**Q6:** What shirt number does Dimitar Berbatov wear?

**Q7:** Who is United's assistant manager?

**Q8:** Who has made more United appearances: John O'Shea or Darren Fletcher?

**Q9:** How many goals did the Reds score during the 2008/09 Champions League group stage?

**Q10:** Which two players scored for United on their Premier League debuts during 2008/09?

**Q11:** Who scored the Reds' only hat-trick of the campaign?

**Q12:** Which four United players scored penalties in the 2009 Carling Cup Final shoot-out?

**Q13:** From which opposing goalkeeper did Edwin van der Sar take the Premier League clean sheets record?

**Q14:** How many games did United lose at Old Trafford during the 2008/09 season?

**Q15:** Which two teams did Sir Alex's men beat to win the Club World Cup in 2008?

**Q16:** Which Red was named the player of the tournament in Japan?

**Q17:** Who knocked United out of the FA Cup semi-finals in April 2009?

**Q18:** Which United player was voted the 2008/09 PFA Player of the Year?

**Q19:** Who scored the Reds' final Premier League goal in the same season?

**Q20:** Prior to defeat against Barcelona in the 2009 Champions League final, how long was United's unbeaten run in the competition?

Answers on Page 62

# Spot The Ball

Use your skill and judgement to decide exactly which is the real ball in this unusual photograph then check your answer with the one on page 62.

# Signed Shirt Competition

Answer the following question correctly and you could win a United home shirt signed by a first team player.

**Q:** *In what year did Sir Alex Ferguson become United's manager?*

Send your entry on a postcard
by 31st March 2010 to:

2010 Annual Signed Shirt Competition
Manchester United Football Club
Sir Matt Busby Way
Old Trafford
Manchester
M16 0RA

(Please include a phone number)

The first correct entry picked
at random will be the winner.
The judge's decision is final.

## Competition terms and conditions

1. Manchester United Limited ("Manchester United") is the promoter of the competition.
2. All individuals correctly answering the question posed (each a "participant") will be entered into a draw and have an equal chance of winning a prize to all other participants.
3. The prize is a United home shirt signed by one member of the first team squad.
4. The prize will be posted to the address provided with the entry. Manchester United is not liable for the acts or omissions of any postal service provider.
5. The competition is strictly one entry per person and all entries must be received before midday on Wednesday 31 March 2010.
6. A draw will be made on or before 5pm on Thursday 1 April 2010 and one participant will be selected at random as the winner of the prize.
7. The winner will be contacted by telephone (depending on what contact info we hold). If we cannot contact the winner within 24 hours of the the winner being drawn (making reasonable efforts), then the winner forfeits the right to the prize and another participant will be drawn as a winner in their place.
8. The draw is not open to employees of Manchester United or their relatives or friends.
9. The prize is non-transferable, and no cash alternative is available. If the winner of the prize drawn at random is unable or unwilling to accept the prize or does not provide the consent requested at paragraph 10 below, subsequent draws will take place until a new winner is found who is able/willing to accept the prize and provide the necessary consent.
10. Each winner (and his/her guardian where they are under 18) will be requested for their consent to the following: (i) for the winner's name to be disclosed to any person requesting that Manchester United confirm the identity of the prize winner; and (ii) for the winner's name and/or photograph to be published for promotional purposes.
11. Subject to paragraph 10 above, details of the competition winners will be made available upon request from Manchester United Interactive, Old Trafford, Sir Matt Busby Way, Manchester, M16 0RA four weeks after the closing date (subject to data protection legislation).
12. Entry into the prize draw confirms your acceptance of these rules.
13. Manchester United reserves the right to refuse entry to, or refuse to award the prize to, anyone in breach of these rules.

# Answers

## Guess The Red

Pic 1 Answer: Dimitar Berbatov

Pic 2 Answer: Jonny Evans

Pic 3 Answer: Ji-sung Park

## Wordsearch

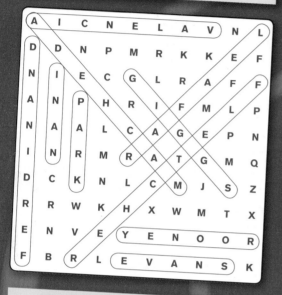

## Anagrams

1. Gary Neville

2. Patrice Evra

3. Nemanja Vidic

4. Ben Foster

5. Wes Brown

6. Michael Owen

7. Anderson

8. Paul Scholes

9. Dimitar Berbatov

10. Michael Carrick

## Spot The Difference

## Spot The Ball

## United Quiz

Q1: Wigan Athletic

Q2: Ole Gunnar Solskjaer

Q3: Serbian

Q4: 1993

Q5: Cristiano Ronaldo

Q6: 9

Q7: Mike Phelan

Q8: John O'Shea

Q9: 9

Q10: Danny Welbeck & Kiko Macheda

Q11: Carlos Tevez

Q12: Ryan Giggs, Carlos Tevez, Cristiano Ronaldo, Anderson

Q13: Chelsea's Petr Cech

Q14: One, against Liverpool

Q15: Gamba Osaka and LDU Quito

Q16: Wayne Rooney

Q17: Everton

Q18: Ryan Giggs

Q19: Darron Gibson

Q20: 25 matches